# FROM PROM QUEEN
## TO HIJABI

# FROM PROM QUEEN TO HIJABI

*My Journey to Faith on a Road Less Traveled*

## U. M. FATIMA

*"Listen to everyone, read everything;*

*believe absolutely nothing*

*unless you can prove it with your own research."*

-Milton William Cooper

"He who does not thank people does not thank God."

-Prophet Muhammad ﷺ

**First and foremost, thanks and praise to God Almighty for everything.**

Thank you to my husband, our children, and my family for your unconditional love, support, and inspiration. I couldn't have achieved anything in my life without you.

Thank you to my friends, teachers, acquaintances, and all those people along the way who have positively influenced my life.

Thank you to my editing crew and book launch team, especially my mom for reading this book one million times.

And lastly, thanks to my husband, mom, and sister for watching the kids so I could write, paint, and complete all the other projects I dive into.

It takes a village!

May God reward all of you, amen.

*"Two roads diverged in a wood, and I-*
*I took the one less traveled by,*
*And that has made all the difference."*
*-Robert Frost*

# TABLE OF CONTENTS

**Author's Note: The Arabic writing 🕌 after the names of the prophets is translated at "May peace and blessings of God be upon him."**

# CHAPTER 1

# "SHE CONVERTED TO ISLAM?!"

They say, "You can't judge a book by its cover," and I am a testament to that fact, a few times over. But I know that it is a human tendency to judge a book by its cover and so naturally the perplexed "*She* converted to Islam?!" question is entirely appropriate in my regards. Growing up and living, in many ways, like a typical American girl and then at 28 years old drastically changing my lifestyle and appearance does warrant a few expressions of surprise by the people who knew me since childhood. I probably didn't seem like the type to adopt an orthodox Muslim lifestyle; actually, I'm sure many people remembered me slightly different than the stereotypical "oppressed Muslim housewife."

Throughout my childhood and into high school, I was athletic and involved in multiple sports, just like my parents were when they were young. As a former college football player and coach, my dad pushed my sister and me to excel at sports and would always have us in the backyard playing catch, often making us throw the softball while kneeling to strengthen our arms. He even prepped me for the Powder Puff football game, making me run agility drills that I'm pretty sure the Patriots do in their pre-season. When I subsequently ran a 64-yard touchdown in the game, he jumped out of his seat with joy and, at that moment, I think he was toying with the idea of sending me to play college football at his beloved alma mater, UNH.

In addition to softball, I played co-ed basketball, volleyball, and soccer from when I was young up into my 20's. I always loved the challenge of competing against the boys. During my last year of high school, I initiated and established the volleyball program in my town, with the financial support of my dad, and was elected the first captain of the varsity team. That program went on to be very successful and was picked up by the town's budget, providing athletes like my sister, who was four years younger than me, the opportunity to excel and earn a volleyball scholarship in college. During that year, I was also the captain of the varsity basketball team, and I participated in the school musical performance as one of the backup singers.

Outside of sports, I was interested in art, fashion design, hair styling, and make-up. My mom had always dressed my sister and me in the cutest outfits when we were little, even if some of the styles were somewhat "fashion-forward," compared to the other kids. I remember one time in middle school; an older student told me that I looked like a "clown" in my purple and blue plaid one-piece jumper with a matching beret. I looked at him, as he was trying to look cool in front of his friends, and said, "Oh! You like that? Thank you!" As I walked away, I muttered, "…ya jerk…" The next week I proudly wore my "clown" outfit again, just to let him know he didn't make me sweat. Apparently, my penchant for fashion was liked by the majority because seven years later, I won the senior class superlative for "best dressed!"

When I was 16, I started working as an assistant at a hair salon a couple of days per week. By that age, I was already a seasoned hair stylist, as I had been cutting women's hair in the neighborhood since I was eight years old. In high school, I would have preferred spending my time styling girls' hair for the school events rather than attend them myself. I skipped the junior prom in favor of doing the hair and makeup for a few of my friends, but for the senior prom, I was determined to make a statement. I looked for inspiration in the magazines, bought some material at Joann Fabrics, and replicated Charlize Theron's orange gown that she wore to the Oscars in 2000. I guess I succeeded at making a statement because I was voted "prom queen" at the end of the night!

Even though I was an honor roll student, but I was always looking for ways to have fun at school. I'd rather not admit it but I was the one putting fake dog poops in the hallway and whoopie cushions under my friends' seats, all in the name of a good laugh. If you saw any spitballs flying across the room, they had probably come from my direction! I wasn't a trouble-maker, but I was definitely in favor of a good time. I wasn't involved in partying or dating, and bullies never messed with me. I'm proud to say that I always spoke up and defended *anyone* who was a victim of bullying, and I couldn't have cared less about what the other kids thought of me for doing so.

# CHAPTER 2

# A FISH OUT OF WATER

S ometimes, however, what I felt inside was different from my external persona. I often felt like a fish out of water: that I was born in the wrong place at the wrong time. I was intrigued by past generations, the wisdom of the elderly, and foreign cultures. When I was a little girl, I questioned the purpose of our existence, why we were here on Earth, who God was, where we came from, and where we are going to after we die. I enjoyed going to church on Sundays because it felt good, even though I had a hard time understanding Catholicism despite years of going to CCD. I noticed that religion was always compartmentalized, reserved for specific times and places, and certainly not an integral part of life for anyone I knew. I didn't like that. I admired the Amish and was curious to know if their God-centered lifestyle was better than our secular one. The day I made my Confirmation in the Catholic Church, I told my mom that my goal was to get to know God better. I would ask Him for forgiveness if I talked negatively about someone or if a friend of mine did, and I felt instinctually guilty if I didn't follow "The Ten Commandments." I was sensitive and mature (except for my humor, of course!), and I hated when my peers acted irresponsibly because it made me feel uncomfortable and nervous. I was a deep thinker, a truth seeker, and very black-and-white in my thought process. What was right was right, and what was wrong was wrong. A lot was going on in my head, but I didn't talk about it with anyone other than my mom.

# CHAPTER 3

# GUT FEELINGS

During my last year of high school, I befriended an international student from Italy who came to study abroad for one year. I took her under my wing and tried to include her in everything I was involved in, in an effort to make the experience memorable for her. We became good friends and spent a lot of time together. She talked to me about her culture and language, and I tried to imagine her little town in the Italian Alps and what life was like in her country. At the end of the school year, she kindly invited me to go to Italy and stay with her and her family for a month. That trip opened my eyes to the world and sparked my interest in foreign languages. In some ways, I felt more comfortable in her culture than my own.

Upon returning home, I began my college career studying Italian at the University of New Hampshire, after having such an inspiring experience in Italy. I picked up the language quickly because my interest was so intense. I would eat, sleep, and breathe Italian, studying day and night. After my first year, I transferred to the University of Rhode Island to combine my interests in Italian and fashion design. But within a couple of days, I realized I had made a mistake. The Italian program wasn't strong enough for me, and I was frustrated that I wasn't in Italy. I finished the semester, hauled it out of there, and two weeks later, I was on a plane to Italy. I enrolled in a six-month study abroad program in Turin through the University of Nevada. I lived with a local Italian host family, and I loved being immersed in the language and culture because it allowed me to fast-forward my learning. When I came home, I applied to UMass Boston because they had a strong Italian department, and it was close to home. I finally found a university that I loved: a strong language department with the diversity that I was searching for. I was able to live at home with my family, work part-time for Alitalia Airlines at the airport, and interpret for US Customs and Immigration. It was a great job experience because I had the opportunity to improve my spoken Italian, as I assisted passengers and worked alongside the pilots and crewmembers. I even had the chance to get to know and translate for Italian celebrities.

Even with having transferred universities four times, I somehow was able to graduate early with a bachelor's degree in Italian studies. I then embarked on a journey of studying everything under the sun. First, I was off to Paris for a couple of months to complete a professional makeup artist course, then back to Boston to attend cosmetology school, which had been a lifelong dream of mine. While studying cosmetology, I became interested in natural medicine after reflecting on the incredible intelligence of "Mother Nature" and her ability to provide us with a cure for most illnesses. Inspired to learn more, I enrolled in a distance-learning doctor of natural health program, which introduced me to many different natural healing modalities around the world. While completing course after course of science and medicine, I finished my cosmetology degree, worked as a hairstylist, and found a little time to travel to the Maldives, rural Mexico, most of the countries in South America, and all of Western Europe. I have beautiful memories and brought home a suitcase full of unforgettable experiences.

After a year of working as a hairstylist in the North End in Boston, I decided to apply to Middlebury College to complete a master's degree in Italian linguistics. When I was an undergraduate at UMass, I remember looking at the brochure for Middlebury Language Schools on the bulletin board in the Italian department, thinking that I wasn't a strong enough student for their programs. But a couple of years went by, and I felt I wanted to take my studies to the next level. Many people asked me why I wanted to continue studying Italian, but I didn't know how to respond. I just had a gut feeling that it was going to be useful to me one day. So, I applied, took the placement test, and received a full scholarship for the master's program! I was elated. I completed half of the program on campus in Vermont and the other half in Florence, Italy. I had so much fun studying at Middlebury, met so many people from all around the world, and had some of the most exceptional professors of my academic career. It was undoubtedly one of the most enjoyable experiences of my life.

After graduating with my master's and, at the same time, completing the doctor of natural health degree, I moved to Albuquerque, New Mexico to attend the Ayurvedic Institute to deepen my knowledge of traditional Indian medicine. I rented a room in the home of a lovely New Mexican woman who helped me settle into life in Albuquerque and introduced me to a lifelong love of sopapillas with honey. I'm convinced that those delectable creations are one of the reasons why people say New Mexico is "the land of entrapment" instead of "the land of enchantment!" We had so much fun together, and we have so many unforgettable memories.

While studying Ayurveda, I, like many of my classmates, became interested in spirituality and its role in healing. In addition to the medicine and science-based Ayurvedic curriculum at the Institute, we studied the Sanskrit language, yoga, the Vedas, and Hinduism. In my downtime, I read books on Buddhism and Sikhism, and I visited temples and ashrams to have practical experiences with different spiritual rituals. I also studied the local Native American culture and became close friends with a dear couple from the Isleta Pueblo (and not just because they made me homemade sopapillas with local honey!) who, still to this day, call me their "adopted daughter."

In late September, my "adoptive" parents invited me to attend a native festival in Taos, and while driving through the rural desert, I saw a small animal running into the lanes of the highway. I told my roommate, who was driving the car to pull over, and I jumped out of the door before she came to a stop. I ran into the middle of the highway and saved a little puppy from getting hit by an 18-wheeler truck. It was like a scene from a movie: I picked her up, ran to the side of the road, and tried to calm her down and comfort her. She was shaking and crying, covered in dirt and ticks, but one look into her eyes and I immediately fell in love with her.

She was the cutest thing I had ever seen. From that moment on, we were inseparable.

Amongst my classmates at the Institute was a Turkish couple who saw that I was interested in studying spirituality. They gifted me a book about the pillars of Islam, and so I carried it around with me to pull out when I had a few free moments. During one of my many trips to the area dog parks in failed attempts to socialize my extremely possessive puppy, I sat down on a bench and started reading the book. After a few moments, I heard a voice say, "If you like that book, I have another one that you might be interested in as well." I looked up and saw a blonde American guy standing in front of me with his two dogs. After chatting for a couple of minutes, I learned that he was an American revert to Islam and was originally from Massachusetts as well! He later introduced me to his wife, who was also originally from Rhode Island, and she subsequently became a very close friend of mine. They brought me to the mosque in Albuquerque, answered many of my questions about Islam, and introduced me to the Muslim community there. I later realized that the whole situation was quite ironic; how dogs and dog parks could bring Muslims (American reverts, of course!) together!

After graduating from the Ayurvedic Institute, my little dog and I drove west to California to meet up with a close friend and then headed east across the country. We landed back in Boston after I was hired to teach Italian at a high school north of the city. The teaching position was especially arduous and time-consuming for me because, a week before school started, they asked me to teach four classes of Spanish to native speakers, a language I had never formally studied! I agreed to do it because I'm always up for a good challenge, and I figured it would be a convenient way to learn another useful foreign language. It was a big undertaking, though, and I felt like I was barely keeping my head above the water. I would teach myself the Spanish grammar lesson the night before the class and then somehow try to make the students understand it the next day. I was surprised at the end of the year when multiple students told me that I was "the best Spanish teacher they'd ever had." Those generous compliments convinced me that I could have a successful career in Hollywood as an actress!

That job, combined with working part-time at a salon in the North End of Boston, enabled me to save up some money for future travel. In the little downtime I had, I continued trying to get to know God by reading and studying different religions and spiritual paths. At a certain point, I decided that I wanted to deepen my studies of Islam, so I began attending an Islam 101 class with a wonderful Egyptian woman at a mosque in Cambridge, MA. I also took private Arabic language classes with a local university professor. I couldn't wait for the Islam 101 class every Monday night to be able to put a scarf on my head and test out what it felt like to be a "hijabi" (a woman who wears a veil and dresses modestly). After the class, I used to keep the hijab on my head while I went food shopping at Whole Foods to see how I felt wearing it in public. Surprisingly, it felt so liberating and natural, and I never wanted to take it off. I used to look for opportunities to wear it, even convincing my mom to attend a few Islamic events with me, wearing hijab and all! I can now officially declare that she would do anything to support me!

One night, while walking my dog on the beach, I asked myself, "If you were to die tomorrow, what faith would you want to die as?" I knew the answer immediately, as I agreed with everything Islam required of a believer: to believe in and worship the One God and to also believe in the angels, the revealed Scriptures, the prophets, resurrection, the Day of Judgment, and predestination. It was the only religion that I agreed with 100% out of all the spiritual paths I had studied. There were aspects I appreciated of all other religions, but there were also some ideas I found to be too man-made because there weren't any original scriptures to verify their divinity. I found verifiable evidence of divine concepts only in authentic Islamic texts, and reliable historical accounts also supported them. I felt confident in my studies and knew in my heart that it was the right path for me, so I knelt down, put my head on the sand, and said the "shahada," or testimony of faith. The moon, ocean, stars, my dog, and of course, God, were my witnesses. My heart was happy, and I felt a huge sense of relief. A week later, I traveled to the first mosque I ever visited in Albuquerque, New Mexico to make my reversion official with my Muslim friends from the dog park as my witnesses. Then, I began slowly making changes in my life.

# CHAPTER 4

# ON THE ROAD AGAIN

pon returning from my short trip to Albuquerque, I began to transition my wardrobe to be more modest, even though I had never worn particularly risqué clothes. If I could have put on the hijab at that point, I would have, but there were only a few months of the academic year left, so I decided to avoid having to explain my personal life to 130 adolescents, and I held off. My students used to ask me why I was wearing long-sleeved shirts in 90-degree weather, and I'd invent excuses like not having a TV to check the weather, in an effort to justify my winter wardrobe in May and June! Thankfully, there were limited hot days before school was released for summer break, so it came just in time for my bad excuses to run out.

I used to search the school for an empty room during lunchtime to use in an attempt to perform the noon prayer. More often than not, someone would suddenly walk in on me, and I would interrupt my prayer and pretend to be searching for something on the ground! I probably looked like I was up to something weird, but little did they know I was innocently trying to pray to God! It was very stressful because I was trying to remember when to pray, how to pray, what to say in Arabic, what it meant in English, and then worry that someone might walk in on me and think I was a crazy person!

Those difficulties made it hard for me to establish consistency in my prayers, and the complications didn't end there. I'd go home from work, hug and kiss my dog, and then worry about how not to get her saliva on my clothes or that the angels wouldn't come around if she were near me. I needed a different living situation to facilitate my life and transition into

"Muslimhood," so in the meantime, I just did the best I could with what I had.

I finished out the academic year and, although I loved teaching, I knew that my efforts and love of working with adolescents would be better put to use in a different environment. So, when summer came, and much to my family's dismay, I packed up the car, grabbed my dog, and I hit the road again, back to Albuquerque. But this time was different. I was there for two days when I had a strong feeling that it wasn't the place I was supposed to be in at that moment. I had a strange feeling that I needed to check out Madison, Wisconsin. I had never been to that state before, and I didn't know a soul up there, but I had heard there was an excellent Arabic program at the University of Wisconsin, so I got back in my car and started driving north.

I pulled into town and stopped at the nearest doggy daycare to drop my puppy off for a few hours while I tried to find the Arabic department at the university. Naturally, they asked me for my contact information, and I looked up and said, "I can't give you much more than a phone number because, at the moment, I'm kind of living out of my car..." The guy looked at me and then glanced at my white '96 Toyota Camry packed to the brim with my belongings and said, "Are you serious?" As I proceeded to tell him about how I came here to study Arabic, a young lady, the groomer, came out from the back room and said, "I was listening to your story, and it sounds pretty crazy. You seem like a nice person, though. If you want, you can try renting a room in my house. I'm going through a divorce, and the house is in foreclosure, so you don't have to pay me much. Oh, and your dog isn't a problem either. I have eight dogs and two cats!" I couldn't believe it. It ended up working out perfectly, and I moved in with her that night. We got along very well and became good friends. It was a great situation for many reasons, but with all those dogs in the house, it was tough to find a clean place to pray. I remember attempting to pray the quick, early morning prayer and becoming overwhelmed by the thought of waking up so early in the morning, getting wet while making ablution, and trying to remove my dog from my bedroom without creating a hoopla with all the other animals in our "mini-zoo!" I felt like it was all too much, so I just rolled out of bed and prayed the quick prayer. I didn't know if it was going to be accepted or not, but I figured some effort was better than just giving up totally. At least I could start by getting used to waking up that early and going through the motions of the prayer. Then, maybe eventually, it would get easier to add ablution and a clean place to pray to the mix.

Within a week, I enrolled in an Arabic course, found a full-time job as an Italian language specialist for a marketing company in Madison, and a second part-time job as a hairstylist at a local salon. The month of Ramadan came, and I was scared to death of fasting, for fear I'd have a hypoglycemic attack and pass out! I had all those common fears of a new Muslim, and I didn't feel comfortable enough to talk about my feelings with someone who I felt understood where I was coming from, and who would be able to push me over those obstacles and fears. So, I skipped the month of fasting, and I felt like I was floating farther and farther away from my desire of practicing Islam.

When I converted to Islam, I expected all Muslims to be like the "believers" described in the Quran, but that wasn't the case. Just about all the Muslims that I met were very kind and generous, but I had higher expectations from them in terms of practicing their religion. I had come to accept Islam after years of spiritual study with the conviction that I had found the truth, so it was disappointing to see born Muslims who didn't appreciate the gift they had been given. From the men, I was expecting to find etiquette that was superior to the rest, so I was slightly disappointed by some of them when they didn't have the "adab" (Islamic etiquette) that I had read so much about. Islam looked perfect on paper, but I wasn't able to find many people who were proud of what they had. I felt like I had found a diamond in the rough, and they seemed more interested in experiencing an American lifestyle. We were going in opposite directions.

Through my disappointment, I realized that Muslims are no different than anyone else. It's an anthropological issue: humans always want what they don't have. It was, perhaps, unfair of me to have such high expectations of the Muslims in terms of practicing their religion. After all, the majority of the people in the world, regardless of religion, would not describe themselves as "religious." I suppose it's as if I expected all Christian men to behave like pastors and all Jewish men like rabbis. I didn't think about the fact that observant Muslims, Jews, or Christians are not the vast majority.

In any case, I was feeling lost and confused, and the thought passed through my mind that I made a mistake by converting. I wasn't looking to get married immediately, but I was 28 years old, and I was trying to figure out what I wanted for my future. There were also many cultural differences between the Muslims from other countries and me, so I felt like I didn't fit together with anyone. I wasn't knowledgeable enough about Islam yet to be able to decipher between a "cultural" Muslim and a "religious" Muslim. I wasn't wearing the hijab at that point, so my physical appearance, coupled with my overly-friendly personality seemed to be attracting Muslims that were not very religious.

Contrary to my appearance, however, I was looking for a very strict, practicing Muslim so that I could grow in faith and benefit from his knowledge and experience. My dad had always told me when I was playing sports, "When the coach stops yelling at you, that's when you should worry." In other words, it's better to have a tough coach who pushes you to reach your potential than an easy coach who lets you plateau and remain stagnant. I applied my dad's advice to every area of my life, from coaches to professors to future partners. I had a strong desire to learn and grow spiritually, but I knew I needed to be somewhat in my comfort zone. Practicing Islam was going to require me to make some significant lifestyle modifications, so I reasoned it would have been a more natural transition if I was already familiar with a potential partner's culture. But that reasoning only left me with two options: American or Italian. I never really considered someone from my own culture, as I had always seemed to feel more comfortable among foreign people. But who had ever heard of an Italian Muslim? I never even considered it a possibility. At that point, thinking that I had possibly made a mistake by reverting to Islam, I started to consider people of other faiths with whom I shared common interests.

Even though things fell into place so nicely for me in Madison, towards the end of the semester, I got another one of those gut feelings that I had to go back to Albuquerque. Again, I had no idea why. I was quite annoyed because I was settling into life there and had met some great friends from all over the world. It was so much fun. I had also just finished a 6-week volunteer training program at a center for at-risk youth, and I wasn't ready to move yet. But I trusted my gut as always, said goodbye to my friends, packed up my car again, grabbed my dog, and drove back down to Albuquerque.

I cried when I got there as I thought I had made a big mistake. I knew I wasn't going to be able to find a situation in Albuquerque like I had in Madison. I was frustrated with myself for not being able to stay still for two seconds, and I was getting tired of journeying. But I knew I hadn't reached my destination yet.

Within a few days of arriving, I enrolled in another Arabic course and joined the "Arabic table" to get more exposure to the language. Amongst that group was a Moroccan girl, who had just moved there as well. We became friends and, after a few months, I shyly told her that I had converted to Islam a year earlier. I was embarrassed to admit that because, even though I tried so hard in the beginning to practice, I lost my momentum and enthusiasm in establishing the five daily prayers and other lifestyle changes. I hadn't met any other converts like myself, and I was feeling lost and alone in my journey. My new friend talked to me about her journey with the religion, invited me to her house for delicious Moroccan food and tea, met with me at coffee shops to help me memorize Quran, and included me amongst her group of friends. She was pulling me back to Islam.

One day while chatting, I mentioned that I spoke Italian and she paused, then looked at me, and said, "Wait a minute. You speak fluent Italian, and you converted to Islam?! I have to put you in contact with someone my family and I know very well in Italy. He's an Italian revert to Islam, and he could help you. I have a good feeling about this."

# CHAPTER 5

# AN ITALIAN MUSLIM

Whata my new Moroccan friend told me about the Muslim revert she knew in Italy, I thought he had to have been an interesting character because I couldn't imagine an Italian man converting to Islam! Convinced it was going to be a waste of my time, I hesitated for a few months to respond to his first email. It was a very confusing time in my life: I had fallen away from Islam, I was trying to survive as a Special Education teacher with a class of boys who were in and out of jail, some drug addicts had just stolen my beloved car, and I was far away from the support of my family. Unsure about everything, I was considering just throwing myself into a career of helping children because it made me feel content. So, I applied and got accepted to UPenn and Tulane University for their master's in social work programs. Then when I realized how much debt I was going to be in after taking out student loans, I decided not to go in that direction. I resolved that my best option would be to return to Madison, Wisconsin, and apply to the Ph.D. program in Italian, which offered free tuition and a stipend in return for teaching courses at the university.

Confident in my decision and subsequent plan, I cashed the $5,000 check the insurance company gave me for my stolen car and walked down the street with my dog to the nearest used car dealership in Albuquerque. I walked in the door with my "guard" dog on a leash, hoping she would deter them from trying to take advantage of a "damsel in distress," and asked to see the newest and cheapest car they had. That ended up being an envy green Scion XB lowrider with tinted windows and a manual trans-mission. It looked like a cross between a Shrek-colored tissue box and a vehicle that belonged in a Cinco de Mayo parade! I figured "beggars can't be choosers" and bought the car. I laughed hysterically as I unintention-ally peeled out of the used car lot with my dog hanging out of the tinted window, barking ferociously at the salesmen. I think I made myself laugh more while driving that car than at any other time in my life! You could hear me coming down the road from far away, the engine revving as I changed the gears. The expressions on people's faces were so funny when they unexpectedly saw a white American girl at the wheel. I'm convinced that this car would have won me America's Funniest Home Video.

Well, my lowrider got me safely to Madison, Wisconsin once again, and I finally responded to his email. It was a long time coming, but that was the beginning of the end. After a few correspondences, I found my-self constantly checking my inbox to see if he had written back to me. I couldn't wait. I thoroughly enjoyed reading what he had to say. After a couple of weeks of email exchanges, we had our first conversation on Skype, and I realized that the direction of my life was about to change indefinitely. We had so much in common on our road to accepting Islam, and we wanted the same future. He graduated from a Catholic seminary and was extremely knowledgeable of all religions, so he was a person who would challenge me intellectually and spiritually. I knew that he had to be an extraordinary person because I had found Italians, in general, to be somewhat narrow-minded. They tend to be very tied to their culture, and differences tend to be criticized more than appreciated. This guy had not only reverted to Islam in the face of adversity, but he was also made fun of and ridiculed by some family members and friends, and yet he was the strongest and proudest believer in God that I had ever met. He had re-tained the parts of the Italian culture that I loved, and he had left behind the parts that I wasn't fond of. Most of all, he cared more about what God thought of him than what anyone else thought. He was the man I had been searching for but didn't think existed. I knew pretty soon after talking to him that I was going to marry him, but I didn't tell him that! The sensible thing to do was to meet in person, but that wasn't exactly easy as we were on opposite sides of the world.

# CHAPTER 6

# NO TIME TO WASTE

He was on the other side of the globe and was much less impulsive than I was. There was no way he was crazy enough to come to America to meet me, but I was more than crazy enough to go to Italy to meet him! So, with my zero tolerance for wasting time, I bought a round-trip ticket to Italy for a few days and went to meet him and his mom.

I landed in Rome, exhausted and disheveled after traveling for 18 hours, but anxious to finally meet this guy I'd only ever seen virtually. He was waiting for me when I came through the doors and gave me a beautiful bouquet of flowers. We shyly introduced ourselves in person and made our way to his car. His mom was waiting in the car and looked at me out of the corner of her eye but didn't move her head. I smiled, trying to get her attention and, when that didn't work, I climbed into the backseat of the car and said to her in Italian, "Hi! It's so nice to meet you!" She barely cracked a smile and said, "Ciao." She was the textbook definition of a typical southern Italian mother. At that point, I was a little intimidated. I knew she was thinking, "Who is this American girl that is interested in my son? And what kind of a girl flies to the other side of the world for a few days to meet a man she's only talked to for six weeks?" She was right, though. In fact, it was hard to convince my parents that it was a good idea to travel all that way alone. I told them that his mom would be there and that I had a friend who spoke very highly of him so, I took a leap of faith.

It was a slightly uncomfortable 2-hour drive from the airport in Rome to their house at the foot of Mount Vesuvius, but when we arrived, his mom was very hospitable. She took me through every room of their elegant home, showing me pictures and special memories of her late husband and the large international company that he founded. I could see she was happy and proud to recount stories from their past and the childhood memories of their three sons. I listened with interest while trying to imagine and piece together how one of her sons (the one I was interested in) grew up and eventually chose a completely different path than the rest of his family. She was a master of southern Italian cuisine, and I stuffed my face for three whole days. I think I even licked the plate after eating her eggplant parmesan! This woman was indeed a tough egg to crack, but by the end of the three days, I think she liked me (although you never know with those southern Italian mammas!)

Spending time in Italy with him, his mom, and some extended family members helped me get to know him better. We were compatible in many ways, but we were also very different in just as many ways. We both had strong personalities, so I knew that we would inevitably butt heads at times, but the positives outweighed the negatives. Conveniently, we spoke each other's language, so that eliminated one difficulty, as we had enough other hurdles to jump over in terms of cultural and lifestyle differences, expectations of each other, and character flaws. We didn't have the luxury of being able to take our time to get to know each other by casually meeting up and chatting over coffee or tea. We were from opposite corners of the world, and one of us would inevitably have to relocate to move ahead with a relationship, so we realized it would come down to "all or nothing" and "now or never." I admired his sincerity and devotion to God and to an Islamic way of life. He was strong, caring, protective, and I found him beautiful inside and out. It felt like our hearts and souls recognized each other right away and that it was our destiny to be together, so we decided to move ahead with an engagement.

# CHAPTER 7

## FACING ADVERSITY

I packed up my bag, said my goodbyes, and he gave me a ride back to the airport in Rome. But we got stuck in rush hour morning traffic, and I missed my flight. That had never happened to me in all my years of traveling. I had a fleeting, irrational thought that maybe it was a sign that I was supposed to stay there with him! Then I thought that maybe God was trying to help me get to know him better; after all, they say you don't know someone until you travel with them! He was very calm throughout the whole fiasco, which was a good sign, and he kindly bought me a flight out the next day. On the positive side, we got to spend another day together, exploring Rome. The next day I successfully boarded the plane, and once I got back to Wisconsin, I sold my Cinco de Mayo mobile and packed up a rental car with all my belongings for one more trip back to Boston. My fiancé was so worried about me driving alone for such a long distance that he talked to me on the phone from Italy the entire way, following me in real-time with Google maps to make sure I arrived home safe. While I thought he was a little overprotective at the beginning, I came to appreciate his sincere concern for my wellbeing. Muslims believe that they are responsible in front of God for taking care of women, ensuring their safety and wellbeing at all times, and I couldn't be more appreciative and grateful to him for taking that duty seriously.

When I got home, I started to see some adverse reactions from some friends and family members when they found out about my quick engagement. Our relationship had begun and developed so fast that I didn't have a chance to explain the situation to many people as things were unfolding, especially since I was living far away from home. I also didn't have the patience to listen to any negative comments, so I only confided in a few people whom I knew would be happy and excited for me. When I started telling a close friend in California about "an Italian convert I met through a friend," she interrupted me and said, "Oh my God, you're going to marry him!" She was dead serious. I chuckled, but I knew she was right.

By this point, I had started to wear the hijab full-time, so my appearance visibly changed. I think that was the change that threw most people for a loop. I had wanted to wear the scarf for a long time, and each day that passed without wearing it felt like a loss to me. With the encouragement of the new man in my life, I put it on and never looked back. Some people asked me, "Could you be a Muslim and just not wear that scarf on your head?" and "Maybe you could wear a hat instead of a scarf?" I responded by saying that I felt good in it and wanted to wear it. I didn't care what people thought of me, but, truthfully, it was uncomfortable seeing people for the first time with it on my head. The ironic thing is that I've seen 80-year-old women walking around with pink and purple streaks in their hair and middle-aged women going to church in miniskirts and nobody bats an eyelash. But God forbid I wear a scarf on my head and dress modestly!

I started to plan my wedding at the Islamic Center in Boston and went to look for a wedding dress with my mom and sister. I couldn't find a modest dress, so I bought one that I liked and then designed and sewed a jacket and head covering using a matching material. I tried not to make it a big deal because I knew that my family and friends were already trying to digest all the changes. I just told them it was a religious ceremony to make us an official couple, nothing legal so not to worry! I minimized the importance of the event: in fact, I didn't even formally invite anyone because I didn't want to put them on the spot and make them feel uncomfortable. I just told my parents to mention it to their families, and anyone who wanted to come was welcome. Truthfully though, a "nikah," is a pretty significant event in a Muslim's life and is usually a "big deal." But in their defense, I was making some drastic life changes: a new religion, a new way of dressing, a head covering, a quick engagement and marriage with some Italian guy they'd never met, then a move to Italy (with my dog in tow) a couple of days later. It was a lot to swallow, but I was confident in what I was doing, and I was sure they would eventually understand one day.

# CHAPTER 8

## A FISH IN THE WATER

A couple of months after meeting for the first time in person, my future husband flew to Boston to meet my family. They all liked him right away, which was a good thing because the day after he arrived, we got married in an Islamic ceremony! My family was happy and supportive of us despite being somewhat discombobulated. Somehow over the years, I think I'd convinced them to trust me with all the crazy things I'd done, so maybe they developed a sort of blind faith, or rather, a blind hope in me, at least! I couldn't have asked for anything more from them. It was the perfect wedding: beautifully simple, humble, stress-free, and sincere in intention. My husband and I brought brunch foods to offer to my family, friends, and other Muslims in the community that happened to be there for the ceremony. I'd recently met two special Egyptian Muslim ladies, who, unexpectedly and so generously, brought a cake, food, decorations, and gifts and made the day so special for us. In fact, since that day, our hearts have grown closer, and we've developed a very special sisterhood. My husband didn't know any Muslim men in Boston at the time, so two random brothers that came to pray at the mosque agreed to be his witnesses and signed off on our marriage! It was also very fitting that the imam who officiated our wedding, Suhaib Webb, is also an American revert to Islam and he made a lovely speech that the non-Muslim attendees could relate to as well. My husband and I knew we were taking a gigantic leap of faith, but we were convinced that if we did things the way God commanded and kept our faith in Him then, God willing, everything would work out (even with a few bumps in the road!)

It was a big jump for me to leave my life so abruptly in the US and to move to Italy. My husband tried to ease my transition by renting a charming apartment for us, complete with all the furnishings (and a full refrigerator!), in a small town near the Republic of San Marino, where he worked with one of his brothers. I met my husband's two brothers and their families after we were already married, and I feel I lucked out. He has two very nice brothers and their adorable families, who all welcomed me as a new member of their family and kindly gave us wedding gifts even though they couldn't be there for the wedding. In addition to my husband's family, the Muslim women in the community came together to congratulate us by decorating our apartment with balloons and decorations, personalized gifts and wedding favors, and a lovely wedding party with attendees from all over Italy. It was all so thoughtful, and we truly appreciated every detail.

I thought that by moving to a somewhat rural, agricultural area of Italy it might be challenging to find a Muslim community nearby, but I couldn't have been more wrong. I ended up meeting many Italian Muslims, who had accepted Islam in adulthood like myself. I actually felt like a fish in the water! I became especially close with a few special women in particular who took it upon themselves to take care of me; including me in Islamic study groups and gatherings, inviting me over for meals and tea, and teaching me about the Italian housewife culture as well. I became a "big sister" to a few special younger girls in the community, and they eventually asked me to teach Islamic Sunday School to adolescent Muslim girls, in Italian of course. I looked back on the last ten years of my life, and I finally realized why God had guided me to study the Italian language. The puzzle pieces all fit together.

I wasn't the ideal Neapolitan girl my mother-in-law always dreamed her son would marry one day, but with time, she admitted that I was like "the daughter that she never had." We went on to develop a mother-daughter type of relationship, arguments and all! Her nickname for me is "Peperina" ("Spicy") because she saw that I am not able to hold my tongue for very long (but neither is she!) I proudly inherited that trait from my paternal grandmother whose grandfather was born in none other than Naples, Italy! There's no way I would have survived my mother-in-law without a trace of Neapolitan blood in my veins! I love my her dearly, but even in her late 70's, she is as quick-witted as someone half her age. In the end, I'm still the girl who "stole" her son, so I have to watch my back, even if I think she loves me!

My transition from a free-spirited American girl to a Muslim house-wife was not always smooth sailing. My husband and I joke that we fought every other day for the first seven years (and we've been married now for 7.5 years!) Talk about "butting heads"! And people think that mark on my husband's forehead is from praying! But with every fight, we grew closer together, thanks to our faith in God. All the fears, worries, and expecta-tions slowly faded away and were replaced with newfound trust and love.

One day recently, years after we got married, with all the challenges overcome and the new ones waiting to arrive, I had a flash that I was finally living out a dream that I once had for myself. I had that dream a long time ago, maybe when I was a little girl, but surely before Islam and before I could've imagined what it would have looked like. All I knew is what it would have felt like. Thanks to Islam, I am living that dream now, and tears come to my eyes as I wonder how I got so blessed. To say "I feel grateful to God" is an understatement for everything He has sent my way, the good and the bad.

I realized that God has mapped out a journey of faith for each one of us. He never promised it was going to be easy and comfortable at all times, and He promised to test our faith along the way. But if we make a sincere effort to get know and remember Him, showing patience and gratitude during the good and bad times, He promised to reward us, here and in the Afterlife. All we have to do is put our trust in Him and hold on to our faith with a tight grip, for it is promised to be a bumpy ride!

# REFLECTIONS

# Searching for God Through the Back Roads of America

Before finding Islam, while living in the depths of existential confusion, I found it incredibly liberating to get in the car with my dog and drive long distances. Like, across the country long distances. I did it four times. My family wasn't at all in favor of these trips, but they knew me, and when I got something stuck in my head, I had to do it. My car was 12 years old, and I had no GPS, just a map with my destination plotted on it. I loved it when I'd drive for hours in the middle of nowhere, and my flip phone got no service. I felt vulnerable and a little bit scared, but that situation made me feel like I only had God on which to rely. I felt close to Him during those moments more so than when I was immersed in the monotony of everyday life. I used to look at the vast sky and talk to Him as I drove, begging him to remove me from the state of confusion I was in and to show me the point of life. It seemed like everyone was content with the typical timeline of; go to school, find a career, get married, buy a house, have kids, save for retirement, retire, and then die. But I found it boring and mundane. Why was I not satisfied with that life? Why did I feel so differently? What was it that I was searching for?

When I graduated from high school, I realized I had a newfound control over the future of my life. Up until that point, things were mapped out for me: wake up, go to school, play sports, do homework, go to bed, repeat. After graduation, I was so confused about what I wanted to do because there were so many choices. I figured my best bet would be to try everything in the shortest amount of time, so I'd have the highest probability of finding my purpose here on Earth. I was very determined and accomplished everything I set out to do, but I got to the point where I felt there was nothing I couldn't do, so I just kept doing more and more, figuring that education was never a waste of time. I felt like I was on a treadmill: running, running, running, but I wasn't getting to where I wanted to be. No matter what I accomplished, I still felt like something was missing. So, I'd eventually lose interest in one subject and move on to next. No situation satisfied me for long before I got bored. I hated being like that.

When I realized that I was insatiable, I started to look towards religion and spirituality for answers. I wanted the answers to all of those questions I had asked myself when I was a little girl. I was 100% convinced that our existence wasn't solely created for the banal purposes of having fun, finding love, having kids, making money, or looking forward to the weekends. I knew there was something more. There *had* to be. I felt I owed it to my future children, if I ever had them one day, to attempt to find out the answers, so they didn't have to wallow in the same state of paralyzing confusion in which I found myself. At the very least, I'd be able to offer them some valid answers to their questions and then let them decide if they want to verify them or not. I worried about how to be a good mother and wife without any divine references or guidelines for how to raise a family. I didn't want to risk investing my time and energy in a marriage only to have it end in divorce because I didn't know how to choose the right type of person at the beginning. Or, risk raising children based on popular principles, devoid of any moral code, that society kindly seems to establish for us and then modify from year to year. I was searching for timeless, divine guidance that wasn't going to go out of fashion, and that didn't have a political agenda. I didn't want to do what the generations before me had done, as I saw many of them make mistakes, never question the status quo, or have the courage to break out of a belief system that they never understood.

Those were the reasons that I went out in search of God. It wasn't necessary for me to leave home and drive around the country searching for Him, as I could have studied the same things in Boston, but I felt a desire to clear my head and reflect, and not be influenced by the opinions of anyone I knew. Ultimately, I achieved my objective, by the grace of God, and accepting Islam was the best decision I ever made.

# DISCOVERING MY TRUE PURPOSE

O nce I became convinced of the authenticity of Islam, I was ready to accept what God said my purpose was here on Earth: to worship Him. It seems so simple, but to worship God means that you put Him first before anyone or anything else, which is actually not so simple. It means that before making any decisions, you first have to consider the laws that God sent down in the Scriptures and the ways of the prophets. Sometimes, these laws and rules clash with your desires, and you have to ask yourself if you are worshiping God at that moment or if you are putting yourself or someone else before Him. This way of thinking requires you to be extremely honest and sincere with yourself.

Even though a new set of rules was a lot to take on, overall, it was a huge relief for me. I no longer had to search for my purpose, wandering through life, studying everything under the sun, just trying to find a sign of why I was put here on Earth. Everything was already mapped out for me. It was humbling because every human being's purpose is the same, and no one is more important than another. A huge weight was taken off my back: all I had to do was follow the directions!

But, to simply "follow the directions" meant I was in for many changes in lifestyle and ways of thinking. Truthfully, just about all of the changes came very naturally to me and felt right in my heart. That didn't mean, however, that they were always easy to implement. Changes take time to digest, and many of them work profoundly on the ego, so there are many layers to peel back and reflect upon.

Before Islam, I was looking for my purpose outside of the house, convinced that it was hiding in a university library somewhere. But Islam reminded me of the importance of a woman as a constant fixture in the home. She has a unique way of providing stability, love, and care to all family members. A Muslim woman is expected to take care of the home and everyone in it, preparing food, and educating the children religiously and intellectually. This immensely important figure, firmly planted in the home, often results in happier and more stable familial relationships. I think of it as a stool: if any of the legs are missing, the stool becomes wobbly and is more prone to fall over. I reflected on this and reasoned that if my true purpose as a Muslim is to worship God, then I should apply His wisdom and proudly take on the role of homemaker to the best of my ability. Muslim women are certainly not forbidden to work, as they are needed to hold important positions in society (female doctors, nurses, etc.) but their responsibilities as a mother and wife should take precedence over a career outside of the home. I reflected on these rules and found them very wise. I didn't think they were oppressive or anti-feminist at all. I felt as if I was an essential player on a team, and for the first time, I felt satisfied and content.

Ironically, I realized I was living out the "typical timeline" that I used to find boring and mundane years earlier! What made all the difference was that I had found my purpose in life, so every action that I made was filled with intention and dignity. This realization was nothing short of miraculous for me because I never imagined that I could have felt so fulfilled without accomplishing something "grand," monetarily speaking. Little did I know that the duties of a homemaker are grander and more rewarded with God than becoming wealthy and celebrated in a career.

At the beginning of our marriage, my husband and I decided that, no matter what our financial situation, I would take on the role of homemaker and home school our children, even if it meant living with less. In this way, I, their mother, can spend the most time with them during their formative years, showing them more love, support, and individualized attention than any other teacher ever could. I can personalize their education to suit their interests while giving them plenty of optional programs to participate in and let them choose who they surround themselves by. They have ample time to explore their interests and spend more time on subjects they love. We organize group lessons, social play, and community volunteering. I feel that this is a very natural and instinctual way to raise and educate children because it is precisely what they do after graduation from high school: design their life according to their interests. Many people say homeschooling shelters children, but I disagree entirely. I believe it's the contrary. I think that homeschooling if done right, teaches children how to: make responsible choices for the direction of their lives, modify individualized educational plans while leaving extra time and space to explore personal interests, and thrive a positive, safe, and loving environment that is necessary for successful learning. I know that many couples feel they both have to work to provide a decent life for their children but, if possible, keeping one parent home with the children is an option worth considering, even if it means having less. When children grow up, they tend to look back and remember more fondly the quality time spent with their loved ones more than the time spent in a big house with lots of toys and possessions, for example.

Even if a woman doesn't have children, being a homemaker is still an incredibly important job. A clean, welcoming environment and home-cooked meals are gestures of love that make a significant impact on the health of a marriage. As a homemaker, with whatever little downtime I have, I study, create, and work from home, making use of the education I acquired years ago. I also engage in hobbies that I love without having to be part of the "rat race" outside of the house, which can often cause a lot of stress on a marriage. Even though a homemaker's work is "unpaid" monetarily, the money that a Muslim woman earns with a part-time job is hers to keep, while whatever a Muslim man makes must be used to support the whole family financially. I think this is a fair trade-off.

# MY BIGGEST CHALLENGE

The lifestyle change that I had the most difficulty implementing was how I treated my dog. Sometimes, I believe we are guilty of humanizing domesticated animals. We treat them like our children: dressing them up, toting them around in baby strollers, and even having birthday parties for them. When I found my dog abandoned on a desert highway, she was only six weeks old. The maternal side of me kicked in, and I felt so sorry for her that I treated her like my biological child. I took her everywhere with me because I felt guilty leaving her at home, even for five minutes. She would sit in the front seat of my car, like a human, and put her paw on my hand as I shifted the gears. We were so connected and loved each other so much, and I believe she understood me on a level that no one else could. I felt protected when I was with her, and she turned into a lion if anyone came close to me.

When I started learning about Islam and that the saliva of dogs is considered impure, that they shouldn't live in the house because the angels won't come in, and that one shouldn't have dogs unless they are needed for security or farming purposes, I was a little put off because I didn't understand why. There is also a hadith (a saying of the Prophet ﷺ ) that says a person loses a mountain of good deeds if one keeps a dog without a valid reason. I understood that God knows His creation better than we do, and He made those rules with wisdom, but I wasn't emotionally able to digest all of that yet. I learned that there are different schools of thought regarding all of the rulings in Islam, but I didn't want to "cheat" and follow one school for the sole purpose of making my life more comfortable with this issue. I talked to many people about this subject, but I never met anyone who had gone through the same situation that I was in. I felt alone in my dilemma, confused about who to believe, and fearful of any "solution" that might remove my dog from my side.

However, I didn't let this problem change my mind about converting to Islam. I had studied Islam enough to know that God's wisdom is so profound, and every rule has a unique purpose. Our human limitations and weaknesses are what impede us from understanding the depth and totality of certain concepts. I also knew that converting to Islam is something that is done step by step, not full immersion because it could "break" a person. In fact, God revealed the Quran in stages over 23 years so that the people could understand, internalize, and apply its prohibitions, commands, and reforms. If it had been revealed all at once, it would have been self-defeating, and the people wouldn't have been able to understand, accept, and apply the rules in an ideal manner. Every new Muslim implements those rules in phases as well, depending on the strengths and weaknesses of the individual. No one should be forced to do anything.

Islam protects animals by giving them their rights as well. As I reflected on God's wisdom, I realized that by not having had His rules to guide me when I first found my dog, I never really let her explore her nature as a canine. I unintentionally taught her that her job was to protect me at all times; therefore, when I wasn't around, she felt lost and sad because she wasn't fulfilling her "purpose." I also limited my own life in many ways and felt a horrible sense of guilt every time I left her. To avoid those feelings, I never left her, creating an ever-increasing dependence on each other. My whole existence was structured around her happiness. But little did I know, she would have been happier if I had honored the nature that God gave her, which was to be outside with other canines in a pack, protecting a property or shepherding animals, etc. I had, albeit unintentionally, created an unhealthy existence for both of us, but I didn't know how to fix it. Actually, I was afraid to fix it. I was afraid to make her sad.

During our first conversation, I discussed this matter with my future husband. It was important to me that he understood my dilemma and that he gave me the space that I needed to make the changes in my own time. He seemed to understand, and he reminded me that "the Quran didn't come down in a day," and that I could take time to adapt. I don't think he understood just how serious I was about that subject, though.

The issue was so important to me that, as a "mahr" (mandatory payment from husband to wife on the wedding day), I just asked for a box of dates from Mecca and begged him to treat my dog well. I couldn't have cared less about anything else.

But, after I moved to Italy with him and saw that the apartment only had a balcony and no yard for my dog, I quickly realized that the dog issue was going to be a bigger problem than we had imagined. He wanted my dog to live outside on the balcony, and my first reaction was, "WHAT??? How about YOU live outside on the balcony?!" Ironically, he ended up being stricter about the dog issue than any other Muslim I had ever met! I felt torn because I knew that his concern was sincere in wanting to follow God's rules, but my timeline was different from his. Although he had dogs growing up, my husband wasn't exactly a "down and dirty" animal lover who didn't mind being covered in dog hair. His mother is meticulously clean and tidy and is always dressed impeccably, like most Neapolitan women, so my husband naturally had expectations that I would be similar to her. My title of "best dressed" in high school apparently didn't carry much weight with him, because he mentioned that when he first met me, he thought I was some lost hippie vagabond, as I traveled around studying and renting rooms in people's houses with a couple of suitcases and my dog. Little did he realize, I too came from a well-to-do family, but I chose to live like that because of my love of studying and adventure.

We were living very different lifestyles. Come to think of it, our first fight (in the car going from the airport to the new apartment in Italy!) started because he was upset that I wasn't embarrassed in front of him to have dog hair all over my pants from hugging my dog after she survived the plane ride from the USA to Italy. I cried like a baby during the whole flight, fearing she was going to freeze and die under the belly of the plane, so I was so relieved and ecstatic to see her come out of the cage alive. The LAST thought on my mind was how I looked at that point, but all my new husband cared about was the dog hair that stuck to my pants! I looked at him and said, "Are you serious?! If I didn't have to put my dog under the plane again to go home, I'd be on the next flight to Boston!" and I think he would have been perfectly OK with that! We somehow survived our first car ride home, and I have to admit that over the years, I have become more like his mom. I realized that I did need a few pointers from her, and she is the best person to go to for "housewife boot camp training!"

My husband had converted to Islam four years before me, so he was more "seasoned" than I was when we first got married. The dog issue caused so much tension in our marriage that we were ready to throw each other off the dumb balcony and put an end to it all! But then we'd pray and ask for patience and the ability to see the other's point of view. It was an ongoing battle for years, but our sincere belief in God was the glue that kept us together during the hard times, nothing else.

Thankfully, the balcony was pretty big, so I was able to transition my dog to spend most of her time outdoors. However, because I felt so guilty for not having her sleep in my bedroom anymore, I took her on really long walks through the Italian countryside to tire her out every day. I have beautiful memories of the times we spent together exploring new places and the random people we met on our walks. One of those random people ended up becoming one of my dearest friends in Italy. I think I have good luck with dog parks because I met her there, too!

On the negative side, my dog and I got attacked three times by other dogs while strolling in public places. After the first episode, when the neighbor saved us from getting eaten alive by an aggressive German Shepherd, I bought pepper spray to keep on my keychain just in case, which I ended up using to save my dog's life a few months later when two Pit Bulls got loose and attacked her from behind. Needless to say, after three major dog attacks necessitating medical intervention in a span of three years, I wouldn't recommend taking leisurely walks with your dog in Italy without some sort of military-grade weapon!

A few years later, when we moved to Boston, I had anxiety attacks worrying about my dog in the cold, brutal weather in the northeast. She always had a warm place to stay and sleep, but it was never good enough for me. I don't think I ever would have been satisfied until she was snoozing on my bed again. I often dreamed of building a two-family house (one side for our family and the other side for me and my dog!) on a farm with other animals. But before I was able to do all that, it was her time to go back to God, crushing my heart into pieces. With all things considered, I tried to make the best of the situation, but it's hard to change roles and relationships between humans and animals after they have already been established. Overall, my dog and I lived a happy life together here on Earth, but I know if we make it to Heaven, it'll be much better.

# LIFE INSURANCE PLAN

s my family and friends watched me make sacrifices for my religion, many of them wondered if I liked to make myself suffer! They saw me try to transition my dog (who was more like a daughter or "doghter" to me) to be an outside guard dog, sweat under a headscarf and baggy clothing in the middle of summer, interrupt whatever I was doing to pray 5 times a day, and fast all day, every day during the month of Ramadan. It was hard for me to explain what the sweetness of faith felt like, which is what drives anyone to make sacrifices for something they believe in.

At the beginning of any journey to faith, lifestyle modifications can seem like sacrifices, but slowly, one realizes that they add so much richness and wisdom to life that they actually become blessings, not sacrifices. To profoundly appreciate something, most of us have to experience the opposite. The depth of gratitude and love that we feel often increases after being put through a difficult test. For this reason, many people agree that a trying situation they've lived through actually made their lives better in the end. God knows what is good for us, much better than we know what is good for us. The Quran says, "Perhaps you hate something, and it is good for you, and perhaps you love something, and it is bad for you. Allah knows while you know not." (Quran 2:216)

When I talk to people of different faiths about their ideas on God and spirituality, many express concepts that they've actually come up with themselves. I've concluded that people do this many times to soften their fear of death or to cope with the tremendous void that is left when a loved one passes away. Insects and strange coincidences become little signs that their loved ones are near, even though these concepts are not present in any of the revealed scriptures. I also noticed that very few people, regardless of religion, take time out of their day to read the holy text of their faith. However, when they are facing death or the death of a loved one, the vast majority of them begin to mention "God" and "praying." Many people instantly become "religious" in those situations, but then when the hard times pass, God is often put on the back burner again, and His name isn't mentioned much after that. Does it make sense that those who make time for God throughout every day are rewarded on the same level as those who don't make any time for Him at all? Interestingly enough, though, the majority of people nowadays pay for a life insurance plan, as if it is going to protect them somehow after they die.

Life insurance is an interesting concept in itself. Insurance is usually bought so that if an unfortunate event happens, there will be coverage to help repair the damage. But death is not an event that might or might not happen. It is definitely going to happen; we just don't know when. Therefore, I feel that preparation for death and what comes after should be a priority in everyone's life and should incur even more immediacy, given the fact that it could happen from one moment to the next and there is no going back. Involuntarily going through the motions of life, following in the footsteps of those who came before us without taking significant time and energy to get to know the Creator, is like buying a low-cost life insurance plan.

Some people believe that there is nothing after death, so they recommend "living it up" now while trying to avoid suffering as much as possible. But what if the Afterlife that the Torah, Gospel, and Quran all describe similarly actually exists? What if all the prophets were right? What insurance policy have we taken out to cover ourselves after death? Wouldn't it be wise to live an enjoyable life, while making sacrifices that benefit us here and now and cover us after we die? Following God's commands is a great life insurance policy option and, better yet, it doesn't cost a dime!

# REFLECTIONS ON THE HIJAB

During my studies of other spiritual paths, particularly Buddhism, I noticed that there is a strong emphasis on the analysis of one's ego. I've participated in many meditations and yoga classes and read several books that were all concentrated on ways to detach from the ego because of how much it influences the mind and the depth of one's spiritual journey. However, many times I find that focusing so much on oneself, without a strong sense of submission to God, can be counterproductive and can cause a spiritual seeker to become even more attached to the ego.

In Islam, while there is definitely a dedicated space for introspection and analysis of one's state of "iman"(faith), many of the prayers, supplications, and reflections are concentrated on God's many qualities, the beauty of His creation, and begging for His guidance, for without it one is truly lost. In short, the importance of the individual believer is dwarfed in comparison to the Greatness of the Creator. The establishment of the five daily prayers and striving to be in constant remembrance of God through the many ways we have been instructed to do so in the Sunnah (sayings and actions of the Prophets) should leave no time for a believer to attempt to invent a new religious practice. Indeed, human innovation is one of the reasons why we have so many spiritual paths today.

In today's society, the word submission often comes with a stigma attached to it, and to be submissive is usually considered a weakness. The present focus is more on the wants of the individual and how to personally benefit from someone or something. But being submissive to the Creator is a wise choice as it brings subtle yet significant spiritual growth to a person's soul. Qualities like patience, humility, introspection, contentment, peacefulness, and satisfaction are some of the benefits of being in submission to God. One learns that everything ultimately comes from Him, so whatever He gives to each person is calculated and intentional. There is a difference between doing one's best to achieve something yet knowing that the result is ultimately up to God, versus taking full credit for achievements and not acknowledging God at all. Hence, the saying of Prophet Muhammad 爨, "Tie your camel and then trust in Allah." In other words, give an honest effort and then trust that whatever the outcome, God is in charge of it. This way of thinking is a test of submission to the wisdom of the Creator and brings immense peace to every result. Being submissive also takes a stab at the ego, as it requires surrendering its desires to those of a much Higher Power.

I have found that the "hijab" is, by far, the best way to practice detachment of the ego for women. It is a pretty big blow to a woman's ego when she begins to wear the headscarf and modest clothing in public because, in my opinion, a large part of a woman's ego is wrapped up in her physical appearance. I believe a woman can have immense "pull" or influence on the people around her just by how she looks on the outside, so when that is removed from her power, it can leave behind some feelings of impotence.

The hijab is often mistaken as the covering of the head only, but the majority of scholars agree that it also includes the modest covering of a woman's "aura" (the entire body except for the hands and face) while in front of men who aren't her "mahram" (father, husband, brother, son, uncle or nephew). A Muslim woman is encouraged to prepare herself while in the house in front of her husband instead of outside the home. This is an interesting concept to ponder. Why have we, as a global culture in the last 60 years, established a norm of looking better outside the house for people we don't know than inside the house in front of a person with whom we chose to spend the rest of our lives? Shouldn't it be the opposite? Maybe that could be one of the many reasons why half of all marriages fail because we spend more time and energy on looking better for men and women who aren't our spouse.

The hijab is not an exclusively Muslim practice; in fact, it is seen in Christianity and Judaism as well. Mary, the mother of Prophet Jesus 爨,

and other pious women in history are always shown with a veil on their head and clothed in flowing dresses. Nowadays, the only women of other faiths who observe "hijab" are Catholic nuns and to some extent, the Amish and Mennonites and some Orthodox Jewish women. There are even Heredi Jewish women who wear the "burqa" (full body covering including the face), which is usually mistaken as an exclusively Muslim practice.

I, strangely enough, was always very attracted to the hijab and modest attire despite my love for fashion and hairstyling, so when I suddenly transformed into a "hijabi," it wasn't as shocking to me as it was to everyone around me. The hijab encourages a woman to stop trying to impress others with her physical appearance. I knew that I wouldn't be young forever, and I found that not wearing the hijab hurt me more than helped me on a spiritual level. Deep down, I, like most people, wanted to be respected for my heart and mind and not for my body. I also realized that I was almost 100% to blame for how I was treated by others, almost solely based on how I prepared myself before leaving the house. Once a person's appearance is toned down and covered, people will begin to judge him/her by what is on the inside instead of what is on the outside. This, however, is easier said than done. The ego does not like to be tamed. It thrives on the attention of any kind and on building up a false sense of importance inside an individual, which can often lead to a distorted mindset and depression in some people.

Even though I sometimes miss expressing myself through my appearance and being on the cutting edge of fashion, the time-sensitive side of me loves wearing the hijab because it makes me feel like I'm working on myself spiritually every day. It keeps me humble, grounded, and focused. My energy is concentrated on aspects of life that I find to be more important than the physical. The hijab gives me more time to think about things like my status of faith, how I can improve or deepen my worship, ways to earn good deeds, etc. It also has given me an overwhelming sense of peace, introspection, and protection, and I feel more respected as a woman.

Some people ask why a man doesn't have to cover as a woman does, and they assume that this has to do with inequality. But how can we compare two totally different genders? A man's "aura" (parts of the body he shouldn't display) is from his belly button to his knee because he has less sexually attractive body parts than a woman. God knows His creation better than we do, and He has assigned different roles and responsibilities to both genders according to their innate biology that He created. Both have strengths and weaknesses, both are given different challenges and responsibilities in this life, and thus, they are incomparable. The only "equal" part of men and women is that they will both be judged and compensated according to their actions.

One of the best things I did after putting on the hijab was moving away from where people knew me for a while. A couple of months after starting to wear the hijab full-time, I got married and moved to Italy. Being able to establish myself as a "hijabi" in a new place where no one knew me previously was incredibly helpful as I got used to my new identity and physical appearance. I didn't have to worry about explaining all the changes I had recently made to anyone because no one knew me before. All of my new friends and acquaintances in Italy got to know me as the "American Muslim girl" and never knew me otherwise. I fit right into a nice community of Italian Muslims, which I never expected to find when I moved to a small town in Italy. That experience strengthened my confidence as a Muslim woman and validated once again that the choices I made were right for me. By the time my husband and I moved back to Boston three years later, I was completely confident and used to my new look and lifestyle. That confidence was essential for me to be able to hold my ground if ever faced with adversity.

# CHOOSING THE "CONTROVERSIAL" RELIGION

Nowadays, Islam is often referred to as "controversial" because it's been unfairly associated with horrible events that have happened around the world in the last 20 years. But who had ever heard of "Islamic terrorism" before the turn of the century? Why, all of a sudden, did it go from a religion of "peace" to a religion of "terrorism"? Why were the same people of Afghanistan called "freedom fighters" by President Reagan during the 1980s and then referred to as "terrorists" by President Bush 20 years later? What happened? I wondered about this and much more, so I began searching for the truth. But what I found while jumping down this rabbit hole was that many pieces of information are not correctly portrayed, or rather conveniently left out, of the mainstream media. This reality is hard for many people to face. Thanks to technology, truth-seeking doesn't require a lot of effort, but it does require being able to accept that many things which have been taught as "truth," may not have been the whole truth, if at all. I've discovered one way to learn the real story about anything in history is to follow the money trail and those who have benefited from trajedies.

The truth is, throughout history, Islam has had a very positive impact on the people and regions that have accepted it. A look into the history of Islam reveals that the religion spread much faster during periods of peace than in periods of war, negating the common myth that it was only spread by the "sword." Muslims are obligated to treat followers of other religions with respect, even when they are in a position to use force. Presently, Indonesia has the largest Muslim population in the world and Islam arrived there peacefully through merchant activities and trading. Here is a short list of some of the Islamic contributions to humanity: the navigational astrolabe, chemical elements and equivalents, the geared gristmill, the first university, the first flying machine, surgical instruments, maps, the oud and lute, the paper mill, tin-glazing, windmills, alcohol distillation, algebra discipline, algebraic reduction and balancing, cancellation and like terms, automatic controls (self-operating valves, timing devices, delay systems), automatic crank, valves, cryptanalysis, ethanol, hard soap, hygienic practices, perfume, kerosene lamp, nitric acid, "syrup", sugar mill, the syringe, the wind pump, Arabic numerals, decimal fractions, the fountain pen, Binomial theorem, Pascal's triangle, Snell's law, drug trials, hyperbolic geometry, mercuric chloride, the steel mill, the weight-driven clock, optic chiasm, the guitar, the metronome, pharmacopoeia, the sundial, coffee, the camera, and thousands more.

From a religious doctrinal point of view, believing in one God, praying only to Him, and following all the same prophets as in Christianity and Judaism is not considered "controversial" by most people. In reality, Islam is a very "live and let live" religion, as the Quran says, "For you is your religion and for me is my religion."(109:6) The Quran teaches that everybody will be responsible for their own actions on the Day of Judgment, and no one will be able to intersect for anyone else. In other words, Muslims are worried about saving their own souls, and they don't win or lose if you save yours.

Many people ask me why I chose Islam, and the reason is so simple: because I found it logical and rational. I found nothing confusing or unverifiable about it, and the original Quran is still intact and has been protected from being modified since it was revealed. In the Quran, I found literary, scientific, and mathematical miracles on every page. It is mindblowing because it contains facts that no one could have ever known 1,400 years ago. It also made sense to me that Muslims are required to believe in all the same prophets in Judaism and Christianity, without putting any of them on the same level as the Creator. Muslims believe that the prophets were all sent to guide human beings back to the right (original) path after they had gone astray. God sent some of them with a divine scripture and sent others without, but they all preached the same message:

believe in the One God and follow the prophets' examples. I appreciate being able to refer to the Quran and Sunnah (sayings and doings of the Prophet of our time) for guidance anytime I have a question about anything.

# "Reverting" Not "Converting"

Many people who come to Islam after belonging to another faith feel that they have "reverted" or "returned" to Islam rather than "converted." This is because Islam, which means "the peace that comes with submission to the Creator," is considered by most to be the first religion of humanity, beginning with Adam. When God created Prophet Adam ﷺ, He taught him to be in "submission to his Creator" or Muslim. There were no other humans on the Earth yet to create and organize other religions so, by default, Islam had to be the first religion. Every prophet after Adam was also Muslim because they were all sent from the same God with the same message: to worship One God and to follow the prophet that He sent during that time.

Muslims believe that children are born with an instinct to believe in their Creator and worship only Him; therefore, Islam doesn't prescribe any infant baptismal ceremony to remove the "original sin" or other rites of passage that indoctrinate children into a particular religion before they are mature enough to make an educated decision for themselves. Muslims believe that each child is born with a clean slate and is entirely innocent until puberty. After that, each person is then responsible for their own actions, and no one is responsible for the actions of another person. Therefore, an innocent baby does not inherit a dirty slate to "baptize" or clean. This is why new Muslims, like me, feel we have "reverted" and not "converted," because we believe we are returning to the religion we were born with.

# "Muslims pray to Allah, not God, right?"

Many people have assumed that, since converting to Islam, I now pray to some sort of mythical god from the Odyssey named *Allah*. I'm sorry to ruin the fantastic imagination of some, but Muslims worship the same God as the Christians and the Jews. *Allah* is simply the Arabic word for God. Many English-speaking Christians don't realize that their Christian brothers and sisters in Egypt, Syria, Lebanon, and other Arabic speaking countries pray to *Allah* as well because they are Arabic speakers.

Here are some more translations of God in other languages: *Dios* (Spanish), *Dio* (Italian), *Dieu* (French), *Gott* (German), *Bog* (Russian), *Zot* (Albanian), *Theos* (Greek), *Jumala* (Finnish), *Shen* (Chinese), *Yahweh* (Hebrew), *Alaha* (Aramaic-the language of the Jesus ﷺ).

All of these names for God refer to the same Creator. So, why do American Muslims, for example, refer to God as *Allah*? The answer is because God revealed the Quran in Arabic, the language of the Prophet Muhammad ﷺ. The Quran is considered by Muslims to contain God's actual words, and in it He refers to Himself as "Al-Lah" ("The God"); therefore, all Muslims believe the word *Allah* is the most authentic name they could call Him. Muslims all around the world strive to learn the Arabic language to be able to read, understand, and memorize the original Quran, which is considered to be a literary miracle, especially because the Prophet Muhammad ﷺ was illiterate. If the original language of a revealed Scripture is lost, people risk eventually misunderstanding the text and not being able to protect it from being modified. God protected the last divine scripture in a second way by requiring Muslims to memorize it and recite it so that, even if all the written Qurans were destroyed, it would never be lost or modified because millions of people all over the world have memorized it word for word. Sometimes we forget that the Old and New Testaments were revealed in Hebrew and Aramaic, the languages of Prophet Moses ﷺ and Prophet Jesus ﷺ. In fact, they never referred to the Creator as God because English didn't even exist during their times. Interestingly enough, Jesus ﷺ called God *Alaha*, which is much closer to *Allah* in Arabic than God in English!

# Muslims believe in Jesus, why don't they celebrate Christmas?"

E ven though Muslims consider Jesus to be the "Messiah" just as the Christians do, Muslims don't celebrate Christmas because they follow in the footsteps of the prophets and are discouraged from inventing new religious practices. Prophet Jesus (peace be upon him) never celebrated his birthday nor the birthdays of the previous prophets, so Muslims are forbidden to do so. The celebration of birthdays comes from Paganism, which was the leading religion of the Romans before they converted to Christianity.

While doing some historical research, I learned that the history of the Christmas holiday began in ancient Roman times when the Church encouraged the Pagan Romans to convert to Christianity to strengthen their numbers for political reasons. Given that the Pagans celebrated the winter solstice around that time, the Church came up with an idea to celebrate Jesus' birthday during the same time so that the Pagans could maintain their celebratory period and would be more inclined to convert to Christianity. However, Jesus was not born on the 25th of December. He was born in the warm months, under a date palm tree. We know that because God told Mary to shake the tree and eat the dates to help her during her intense labor. Dates are ripe in the summer, not in the dead of winter.

# "WILL YOU RAISE YOUR CHILDREN AS MUSLIMS?"

When I reverted to Islam, I chose the religion that I thought would give me the best guidance for living this life and the best chance of achieving a good seat in the Afterlife. Like all mothers, I want the best for my children and would do anything for them. I feel that raising my children as Muslims is the greatest gift I could ever give them. However, when they hit puberty, it will be time for them to decide if they would like to continue in the Islamic faith or choose another spiritual path, if any. As Muslims, we believe that there is "no compulsion in religion" (Quran 2:256) so no one can force another to believe against their will. Of course, my husband and I pray that our children will follow in our footsteps, but we are fully aware that we ultimately have no control over that decision, God does. We respect our parents for accepting our decision to choose a different religion than that of our forefathers, and we will show the same respect to our children for whatever decision they make.

# My Journey to Faith on a Road Less Traveled

I realize that my journey to faith has certainly been a road less traveled. It was a journey filled with adventure, intuition, determination, confusion, courage, and ultimately, achievement. Since I was a little girl, my mom always taught me to "be true to yourself" and to "love yourself," two lines that she eventually became known for in her career as an elementary school counselor. She lovingly drilled those lines into my sister's and my head so many times that I think we never knew how not to love and be true to ourselves! Whether or not my mom realized back then that I would have taken those lines to the next level and become an orthodox Muslim, is another question!

While I do believe our purpose as humans is the same here on Earth, I am sure that God has a different plan for every single one of us. There have never been two people who have lived the same life, so following the advice of another person instead of divine guidance can lead one astray. We all have the responsibility on our shoulders to intuitively swim through this ocean of life, as we will all die alone eventually, the same way we were born. Our lives are full of ups and downs, but in the end, it is all just a test. We are being tested during good times and tested during bad times. We each have been dealt a different hand of cards with divine intention, and we are being watched as we try to win our own game.

I feel so grateful for having been able to cultivate the qualities of self-confidence, self-love, and determination at a young age because it makes being "true to yourself" a whole lot easier if your journey requires you to swim against the tide. While I am truly blessed to have a family who always supports me albeit not sharing my same beliefs, I believe that developing a strong relationship with God will strengthen anyone, even those who may not be lucky enough to have a strong support system around them. I could never have achieved anything of real value in my life without the strength to stand up for what I thought was right, even when I couldn't see the road ahead of me. It can be scary to change, but if we are truly sincere in our intention and fear the outcome a little bit less than we fear God, He will always guide us to the right path.

**"Take one step towards Me, I will take ten steps towards you.**

**Walk towards Me, I will run towards you."**

**-God Almighty (Hadith Qudsi)**

Did you enjoy reading this book?

I would genuinely appreciate it if you'd leave a review on Amazon!

Thank you so much!

Please visit me on my website at www.umfatima.com and sign up to receive occasional email updates from me whenever I have something new coming down the pike!

Thank you for reading and may God bless your journey.

U.M. Fatima :)